# All THINGS RACCOONS For Kids

FILLED WITH PLENTY OF FACTS, PHOTOS, AND FUN TO LEARN ALL ABOUT RACCOONS

ANIMAL READS

AR
WWW.ANIMALREADS.COM

# THIS BOOK BELONGS TO...

_____

_____

WWW.ANIMALREADS.COM

# A SNEAKY MAP OF WHAT'S INSIDE

Nature's Clever Masked Explorers! ........... 1

What Makes a Raccoon *a Raccoon*? ........... 7

Dressed Like a Superhero ................... 13

Raccoon Hideouts Around the World ........ 29

Tasty Treasures ........................... 37

The Amazing Journey ....................... 47
   *of Growing Up Raccoon!*

Super Cool Facts .......................... 57
   *That Will Blow Your Mind!* ...................

Congratulations! .......................... 65
   *You're now a Raccoon Expert!*

Thank You! ................................ 69

# NATURE'S CLEVER MASKED EXPLORERS!

Have you ever heard mysterious rustling in your backyard at night? Maybe you've seen a striped tail vanish behind a trash can. Or perhaps you've spotted a funny furry face with a black mask peeping at you from a tree. If so, guess what? **You've met a raccoon!**

Raccoons may look like mischievous bandits, but these animals are special. With their dark face masks, bright eyes, and busy little hands, raccoons make us smile with their silly antics. These masked creatures have amazing superhero skills! Their dark masks aren't just for looking cool—they actually help raccoons see better at night by cutting down glare, kind of like sunglasses that work in the dark.

The real wonder of a raccoon is in their hands. Raccoons have some of the most amazing hands in the animal world. They can unscrew tight jar lids, open latches, and even figure out locks! A raccoon's hands are filled with special nerve endings—

tiny parts that feel things—making their touch super sensitive. It's almost like they can "see" objects just by touching them!

Did you know raccoons can remember how to solve puzzles even after three years have passed? That would be like you remembering how to solve a tricky game you played when you were much younger!

That's right: these little masked adventurers are some of the **world's smartest, sneakiest, and most adaptable animals**. Adaptable means they can live and thrive in many different places. With their

clever hands, problem-solving brains, and ability to make homes almost anywhere, raccoons are nature's survival champions.

You're about to discover amazing raccoon secrets! You'll learn how their striped tails help them stay balanced on branches and keep warm in winter. We'll explore why they dip food in water before eating (no, they're not washing it!). You'll find out how baby raccoons—*called kits*—learn all the skills they need. We'll see why city raccoons are often smarter than forest raccoons and how these clever animals have made homes everywhere, from deep woods to busy streets.

Are you ready for a raccoon adventure? You'll learn how they climb trees headfirst, why they love nighttime, and what makes them so clever. By the end of this book, you'll see raccoons in a whole new way!

So grab your flashlight—raccoons are night adventurers, after all! And don't worry if you can't see in the dark—our raccoon friends will lead the way!

# DON'T JUDGE A RACCOON BY ITS MASK!

# WHAT MAKES A RACCOON A RACCOON?

**R**accoons belong to a special group of animals that scientists call **mammals**—*but what exactly does that mean?*

Mammals are different from other animals in some *really cool ways.* While snakes have scales and birds have feathers, mammals have **fur or hair** to keep them warm. Lizards need sunshine to warm up, and fish are as cold as the water around them, but mammals can **keep their bodies warm** no matter the weather. And here's something *amazing*—while birds and reptiles lay eggs, **mammal babies are born alive!** Baby raccoons don't hatch from eggs like baby birds or turtles do. Instead, they're born tiny and helpless, drinking milk from their mothers, just like human babies, cats, dogs, and many other animals.

## WHY DO SCIENTISTS GROUP ANIMALS INTO DIFFERENT FAMILIES?

Scientists like to be very organized with their research. *Maybe you're the same way with your toys! Perhaps you sort your stuffed animals into different "families," too. You might put all the scaly ones, like lizards and snakes, in one group. Then you'd gather all the feathered ones, like birds, into another group. And finally, you'd have the furry

ones—like bears, cats, dogs, and, of course, **raccoons**! Grouping similar animals together helps scientists learn more about each type of animal.

Just like your family has a special last name, raccoons also have their own scientific family name. Scientists call this family **Procyonidae** (say it like this: pro-see-ON-ih-day). *Don't worry if you can't say it perfectly*—even some scientists have trouble with that one! This family includes some interesting cousins, like **coatis** (which look like raccoons with super-long noses) and **ringtails** (think of a cat with a striped tail as long as its whole body!). But among all these furry relatives, raccoons might just be the *smartest of them all*.

Scientists also put raccoons into a smaller group still, called **Procyon**, which comes from the Greek word meaning **"before dog"**. *Kind of a weird name, right?* After all, raccoons aren't related to dogs at all! It would be like someone calling you *"before elephant"* just because you both like peanut butter. Sometimes, scientists choose some pretty funny names, but they all help us understand how different animals are connected.

Ready to discover even more amazing things about these masked masterminds? Hold onto your hiking boots because next up, we're exploring all the superpowers that make raccoons the sneakiest problem-solvers in the wild. You won't believe some of the clever tricks they can do!

# KEEP CALM
## AND RACCOON ON!

# DRESSED LIKE A SUPERHERO

## AMAZING RACCOON FEATURES!

If raccoons starred in a superhero movie, they would be showing off some remarkable powers! Every part of a raccoon's body has a special ability, from their mysterious black masks to their super-sensitive hands.

Let's explore what makes these nighttime adventurers so incredible—from head to tail!

## THE MASK OF MISCHIEF

Superheroes wear masks to protect their identities, but raccoons? They wear theirs to see better at night! That black mask isn't just for looking cool (though it definitely does the trick)—it actually helps raccoons see more clearly by **reducing glare**. It works like the black stripes athletes wear under their eyes during sunny games. The dark fur soaks up extra light that might make it hard to see. *Imagine*

*having built-in sunglasses that also help you see better at night*—that would be pretty awesome, right?

And here's something truly remarkable: **no two raccoons have the same mask pattern!** Just like people have unique fingerprints, each raccoon's mask is special. Scientists can tell different raccoons apart just by looking at their masks, that's the easiest way to track them.

## FINGERS THAT CAN FEEL THE WORLD

If raccoons had a signature superpower, it would definitely be their extraordinary hands. Imagine

having hands so sensitive that you could "see" things just by touching them—that's precisely what raccoons can do! Their paws have special nerve endings that send detailed information to their brains. Nerve endings are tiny parts that feel things. These nerve endings are so sensitive that raccoons can tell an object's shape, texture, and temperature just by feeling it. And here's the *best part*—they become even more sensitive when their paws get wet! That's why raccoons often dip their food in water. They're not washing it—the water helps their paws "see" the food even better.

These *fantabulous* hands can do even more tricks. Raccoons can untie knots, unscrew jar lids, and pick up tiny objects as small as a rice grain. Their fingers move so well that they can feel the difference between similar objects. They can tell when

it's a juicy crayfish and not a slippery rock in a stream. Scientists think raccoons use their hands almost as much as their eyes to explore. When a raccoon finds something new, it first touches it all over to figure out what it is—kind of like a blind person reading a book in braille.

## A TAIL FULL OF TRICKS

A raccoon's striped tail is a **multi-tool** that helps them do all sorts of things! First, it acts like a built-in balance beam. It helps raccoons stay steady when they walk on narrow branches or fences. If they start to wobble, they shift their tail to the other side, *just like a tightrope walker using a balancing pole!*

 ALL THINGS RACCOONS FOR KIDS

Their tails also work as cozy blankets. When raccoons curl up to sleep, they wrap their long, fluffy tails around themselves to stay warm. It's like having a built-in sleeping bag! And those black and white rings on their tails? They help raccoons spot each other in the dark or in tall grass! Baby raccoons, called **kits**, follow their mother's tail, which acts like a striped flag leading the way.

## MORE SURPRISING SECRETS: FROM HEAD TO TOE!

Raccoons have an impressive set of **whiskers** that do more than just look cute. These whiskers can

These whiskers tell me everything!

feel the tiniest changes in air movement. This helps raccoons sense everything around them, even in complete darkness. Their whiskers are so good that a raccoon can tell if it'll fit through a tight space just by touching its snout against the opening. Just like cats, they have a *built-in measuring tool* on their faces!

Their fur is another clever feature. Raccoons have special **double-coated fur** that keeps them warm and dry. The outer layer is thick, rough, and waterproof, like a raincoat. Under that is a layer of softer, thicker fur that traps heat. This keeps them cozy, even on cold winter nights. Their special coat lets raccoons swim in cold water and explore snowy forests without feeling too cold.

Raccoons also have **sharp claws** that are always ready for action. Unlike cats, which can pull their claws in, raccoons' claws are always showing. This gives them a strong grip for climbing trees, digging for food, and holding onto tricky objects. Their claws are so sharp that raccoons can even climb down trees headfirst—*something most animals can't do*!

And let's not forget their **eyes**, which work like built-in night vision goggles. Behind each raccoon's eye is a special mirror-like layer called the **tapetum**

Shine a flashlight at me at night, and you'll see my eyes glow green!

**lucidum** (say: tah-PEE-tum loo-SEE-dum). This layer bounces light back through the eye. This gives their brains a second chance to see what's around them. Have you ever seen how a raccoon's eyes glow bright green when you shine a flashlight at them at night? That's the tapetum lucidum working! It helps raccoons find food, spot danger, and see obstacles in the dark, making them excellent nighttime explorers.

With superhero masks, super-sensitive hands, and night-vision eyes, raccoons are perfectly built to explore the world after dark!

## BEHIND THE MASK: THE SECRET LIFE OF RACCOONS

With all their amazing features, you might think raccoons strut around the animal world like show-offs, but they're more like curious scientists mixed with playful acrobats! Let's peek behind those masks and discover what raccoons are really like.

First up, something that will surprise no one: raccoons are incredibly curious creatures. If they had a motto, it would probably be **"If it exists, we must investigate it!"** This endless curiosity is one of the things that helps raccoons survive in all sorts of places. We already know these masked explorers are super bright, but just *how* smart are they? Scientists have discovered that raccoons can remember how to solve puzzles years after figuring them out just once! We know that raccoons can open complicated locks, figure out multi-step problems, and even remember which garbage cans have the tastiest treats (*much to the frustration of many humans!*).

Most raccoons are **solitary animals**, so they prefer to spend time alone. Solitary means they like to be by themselves. Unlike penguins huddling together in big groups, raccoons are more like solo adventurers, sneaking through the night alone. But don't be sad: they're not entirely alone all the time. Sometimes, on especially cold winter nights, raccoons **share their dens** with other raccoons to stay warm. It's like having a cozy winter sleepover—but only when it's super cold!

And when it comes to communication, raccoons are quite the chatterboxes! Believe it or not, raccoons can make **over 200 different sounds.** They can purr like cats, chirp like birds, whistle like kids at recess, and even make noises like tiny horses! Each sound has its own special meaning. One sound might say, **"This food is delicious!"** while another might warn, **"Watch out! Danger nearby!"** And, of course, baby raccoons have their own unique way

This raccoon mom and her three little ones are out berry picking... and probably chattering the whole way!

of calling for their moms—like saying, **"Mom, where are you?"**

Raccoons are extremely **adaptable**—which means they're great at changing to fit new places and situations. In forests, they might be shy and avoid people. But in cities, raccoons become a lot braver! Some city raccoons have learned that porches, garbage cans, and gardens often hide super tasty treats. They've even figured out how to open containers, sneak through small gaps, and climb fences to get to the good stuff. Most raccoons are **nocturnal**, which means they're active at night when we humans are sleeping. But some city raccoons have learned that coming out during the day means *more snacks*—so they break the rules and adjust their schedules!

And while raccoons usually prefer to work alone, they're not above teaming up when it comes to sneaky missions. For example, it's not unusual to see one raccoon distracting a dog guarding a yard while another sneaks in to grab the food. What clever teamwork!

Raccoons might not be party animals that hang out in big groups, but they're definitely some of nature's most interesting characters. They're curious, clever, and always ready for an adventure—especially if that adventure involves solving puzzles or finding snacks!

# WHY DON'T RACCOONS EVER GET CAUGHT STEALING?

**They always wear a mask!**

# RACCOON HIDEOUTS AROUND THE WORLD

## RACCOON HOMES

By now, we know that raccoons can live almost anywhere—deep in a forest, tucked into a city attic, or sneaking snacks from a backyard porch. These clever critters are experts at finding the perfect spot to settle down, no matter where they roam.

In the wild, raccoons prefer areas with tall trees. Trees give them shelter from rain and snow, safe places to sleep during the day, and quick escape routes when danger comes around. With their amazing climbing skills, raccoons can climb tree trunks like furry little mountaineers. They turn hollow branches and cozy nooks into perfect homes. Fallen logs and spaces between large rocks also make great dens. If another animal leaves behind an empty burrow, a raccoon might move right in—no moving trucks needed!

I love my cozy little home in the woods!

City life gives raccoons even more choices. While most wild animals stay away from busy streets and noisy neighborhoods, raccoons have found that human homes and buildings have plenty of hiding spots—*and even easier meals.* Chimneys keep them warm during cold nights. Attics can be quiet places to raise their babies. Porches, decks, and sheds also make excellent hideouts. These spots offer dark, quiet, and protected spaces to rest during the day. When the sun sets, raccoons are ready to sneak out and explore the neighborhood, looking for tasty snacks.

Once upon a time, raccoons lived only in North America. You could find them from Canada's snowy forests to Panama's warm beaches. But thanks to their adventurous spirit—and some help from humans—raccoons have become world travelers. In the 1930s, people brought raccoons to Germany. They thought raccoons might make good pets or could be raised for their soft, fluffy fur. A few escaped into the wild, and soon, raccoons were exploring forests and cities all across Europe. Today, you can find raccoons not just in Germany but also in France, Poland, and even as far east as Russia!

Hey! This is my time to be up—and your time to be in bed!

Yeah... I can pretty much live anywhere!

A similar story happened in Japan during World War II when raccoons were brought as pets. But as many people quickly learned, raccoons aren't the easiest houseguests. They're curious, mischievous, and too good at opening cabinets and exploring places they shouldn't go. Some raccoons escaped, while others were set free. Before long, they had spread across the Japanese countryside. Now, you can see raccoons wandering through forests, exploring city streets, and even sneaking into ancient temples and shrines looking for food.

No matter where they live, raccoons always need a few key things to feel at home. First, they need

fresh water for drinking, finding food, and making their sense of touch better by dipping in their hands. Food is just as important, whether it's berries and nuts in the forest or leftover takeout in a city garbage can. And, of course, raccoons need a safe, dark place to sleep during the day. This might be a hollow tree, a rocky cave, or the cozy space under a porch.

Whether they're climbing trees in a Canadian forest, exploring city streets in New York, or sneaking through ancient temples in Japan, one thing is for sure: raccoons know how to make themselves at home wherever they go!

# TASTY TREASURES

## HOW RACCOONS FIND THEIR FAVORITE FOODS

Now that we know raccoons really can make themselves at home just about anywhere, you might be wondering—what do these clever furballs actually eat? Well, get ready for a surprise (or not!) These masked munchers aren't picky eaters at all. They're what scientists call **omnivores**, which means they eat both plants and animals. So, a raccoon's menu can include a little bit of everything—berries, fish, bugs, pizza crusts, and even leftover burgers. *Sounds a bit like us humans, right?*

## DINNER IS SERVED: FOREST EDITION

Raccoons are expert treasure hunters in the wild, always searching for the next tasty snack. On the forest floor, they sniff out fallen berries, crunchy acorns, and mushrooms, using their fingers to check if the food is ripe and ready to eat. Their sharp

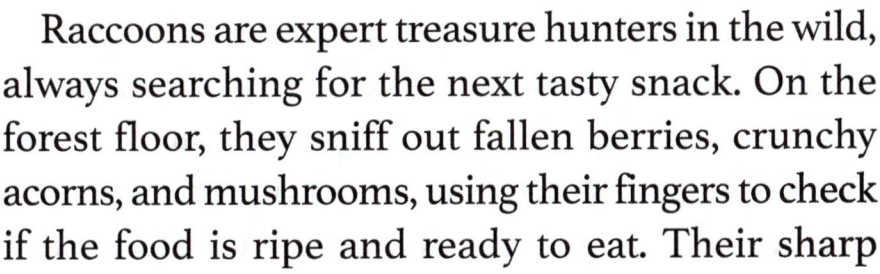

noses help them find hidden treats like nuts buried in the soil. Their nimble hands let them dig up insects and worms that other animals might miss.

But the forest buffet doesn't stop on land! Raccoons also love to wade into shallow streams and ponds, where their hands act as underwater treasure detectors. Without seeing what's beneath the surface, they can feel around for slippery fish, quick-moving crayfish (like tiny lobsters), and squishy frogs. Raccoons can catch their dinner with amazing speed using their hands like built-in fishing nets.

There's usually food up here...

And when they get hungry higher up in the trees, raccoons collect bird eggs or fruit like apples and pears. Their sharp claws and strong grip make them excellent climbers. They can climb tree trunks and branches as quickly and easily as we climb stairs. Whether they're exploring the ground, wading through water, or climbing high into the treetops, raccoons know exactly where to find the tastiest snacks.

## TAKEOUT TIME: SNACKS IN THE CITY

Just as raccoons have mastered finding food in the forest, they've also learned to snack their way through cities and suburbs. With their clever tricks,

they've figured out that humans leave all kinds of treats just waiting to be discovered. Garbage cans become all-you-can-eat buffets, garden trees offer juicy fruits, and pet food left outside is an easy and *delicious* midnight snack. To a hungry raccoon, exploring a backyard or city alley is like finding a treasure chest full of tasty surprises!

Some raccoons remember which houses put their garbage cans out on which nights. Others learn that visiting certain restaurants after closing time might mean finding some yummy leftovers. With their problem-solving brains and quick fingers,

Leftover pet food? Yeah… that's ours now.

raccoons can even figure out how to open lids and containers that other animals couldn't open.

Whether digging for grubs in the forest, fishing in a stream, or sneaking snacks from a backyard garbage can, raccoons know how to find food wherever they go. Their curious nature, clever minds, and sensitive hands make them some of the best food hunters in the animal kingdom!

## ESCAPE ARTISTS: HOW RACCOONS OUTSMART THEIR ENEMIES

Even the cheekiest raccoon knows to steer clear of great horned owls!

Finding food isn't always easy—or safe. Raccoons have to watch out for animals that might see *them* as a tasty meal. These animals are called **predators**, and raccoons have several dangerous ones to avoid in the wild.

One of the sneakiest is the **great horned owl**. With their silent wings and sharp talons (powerful claws), these night hunters can swoop down without making a sound. They often target defenseless young raccoons who wander too far from their

Zoom! You'd be surprised how quick I can move!

mothers. That's why raccoon moms are extra protective of their kits, teaching them to stay close and listen for danger.

On the ground, raccoons have to watch out for **coyotes** and **wolves**, who hunt raccoons if they get the chance. But raccoons have a few tricks up their furry sleeves! Since they're expert climbers, they often build their dens high up in trees where ground predators can't reach them. And if danger appears while they're out exploring, raccoons can

Just because I'm lounging doesn't mean I'm not on guard.

dash up a tree in seconds—*faster than most predators can follow*!

Raccoons also use their natural smarts and built-in tools to stay safe. Since they mostly explore at night, they tend to search for food when many predators are asleep. Their super-sensitive **whiskers** also work like tiny security alarms, detecting even the slightest movements in the air. If a predator sneaks up while a raccoon is busy investigating its next snack, those whiskers send a clear warning signal—it's like having motion detectors that set off alarm bells!

So, whether they're munching on forest berries or snacking on city leftovers, raccoons always keep one eye (and a few whiskers) on alert. After all, even nature's cleverest bandits need to be careful!

# WHAT'S A RACCOON'S FAVORITE SNACK?

**Whatever you left out!**

# THE AMAZING JOURNEY
## OF GROWING UP RACCOON!

Every raccoon's life is an adventure, starting as a tiny, helpless kit and growing into one of nature's cleverest nighttime explorers. Just like you've grown from a baby into who you are today, raccoons undergo incredible changes as they grow up. Let's follow these masked bandits as they transform from candy bar-sized babies into skilled adventurers!

### TINY POTATOES WITH MASKS: BABY RACCOONS' FIRST WEEKS (0-2 MONTHS)

When raccoon kits are born, they weigh just **two to three ounces** (about 60-75 grams)— *that's lighter than a candy bar!* Their eyes are shut, their fur is thin, and their pink hands look like tiny mittens. They can't see, hear, or walk at this stage, so they snuggle safely in their den while their mom keeps them warm and protected.

Pictured here are some rescued kits—they're growing more fur each day, but still need lots of care!

Mother raccoons choose their dens carefully. The perfect nursery is a cozy hollow tree, a hidden cave, or a snug space between rocks. Sometimes, a raccoon might even move into the attic of a house. As the weeks pass, the kits grow quickly. Around three weeks old, their eyes open, and their first tiny teeth poke through. Their famous black masks appear, and their fluffy striped tails begin to grow. By the time they're eight weeks old, these once-wrinkly little potatoes have transformed into miniature raccoons, ready to explore the world outside their den!

ALL THINGS RACCOONS FOR KIDS　　49

Watch out, world! This little explorer is on the move!

## WOBBLY FEET AND WILD ADVENTURES: LEARNING TO BE A RACCOON (2-12 MONTHS)

The kits are ready to take their first steps outside at two months old. At first, they are a bit wobbly, like you might be the first time you try walking on a tightrope, but practice makes perfect! Soon, they're climbing, balancing, and exploring with growing

confidence. Their mom acts as teacher and bodyguard, watching them tumble and stumble through their first adventures.

At around three months old, the kits begin learning how to find food. Their mom shows them the best spots to search—wading into streams to feel for fish, climbing trees for bird eggs and fruit, and digging in the soil for crunchy insects and nuts. Their sensitive hands become their *secret tools*, helping them explore the world through touch.

But finding food isn't their only lesson. The kits also learn how to climb trees quickly when danger comes near, which foods are safe to eat, and how to explore quietly without being noticed. They discover the best places to sleep, stay warm, and how to open lids and sneak into tightly sealed containers!

## MASTERS OF THE NIGHT: LIFE AS AN ADULT RACCOON

After a year of learning and growing, young raccoons are ready to head out on their own adventures. By this time, they've grown from tiny kits into full-sized raccoons, weighing anywhere from 10 to 30 pounds—that's about the size of a large house cat! Their thick, fluffy fur makes them look even bigger, giving them that classic round, huggable shape (though they're a little too mischievous to be cuddly pets!).

Psst... We're a year old! Time to act like adults... or at least try...

Life in the wild isn't easy, and most raccoons live for about two to three years. That might not sound very long, but when every night is an adventure, it's a life full of excitement! Some raccoons, especially those who stay safe from predators and find plenty of food, can live up to five or six years. And for raccoons living in zoos or wildlife sanctuaries—where they're protected and well-fed—life can be much longer. Some of these lucky raccoons have

ALL THINGS RACCOONS FOR KIDS  53

I'm teaching this little one everything I know!

reached **20 years old**! That's like a human living to be 100, which is pretty impressive for a little masked bandit.

Female raccoons usually have babies every year, in spring. They typically have three to five babies at a time, though some might have even more! Like their mothers, they find a safe, cozy den and spend the next year teaching their kits everything they need to know about life as a raccoon.

With all the skills they learned as kits—climbing, swimming, finding food, and staying safe—adult raccoons become true masters of their world. They know the best places to find food in every season, which garbage cans are easiest to open, and where to find the coziest sleeping spots. Their quick minds and busy hands help them solve problems and get past obstacles that would stop most other animals.

It's pretty amazing to think that these clever, curious animals start out as tiny, wrinkly kits no bigger than a candy bar. From their first wobbly steps to their midnight adventures as adults, raccoons prove that they're some of nature's most remarkable survivors—intelligent, adaptable, and always ready for their next great adventure!

# WHAT'S A RACCOON'S FAVORITE GAME?

## Hide & Squeak!

# SUPER COOL FACTS
## THAT WILL BLOW YOUR MIND!

Think you now know *everything* about raccoons? Hold onto your hat—these facts are guaranteed to make you say, *"No way!"* and rush to tell everyone you know. Get ready for some wild raccoon trivia that proves these masked adventurers are even more impressive than you thought!

### SUPERSTAR ATHLETES IN FUR COATS

Raccoons might look a little round thanks to their fluffy fur, but don't be fooled—they're built for action! These speedy critters can **run as fast as 15 miles per hour (24 kilometers per hour)** to make a quick getaway if needed. And when it comes to jumping, raccoons will surprise you with some serious skills—they can leap from heights of **40 feet (12 meters)** without getting hurt. That's like jumping off a four-story building! Plus, raccoons are strong swimmers. They can paddle through rivers,

ponds, and streams for up to **three hours** without a break. Talk about staying afloat!

## THE POWER OF COZY NAPS

While bears snooze all winter long, raccoons have a different game plan. When it gets really cold, they take long naps that can last for weeks, only waking up on warmer days to search for food. This special kind of winter sleep is called **torpor**. During their chilly snoozes, raccoons can use up to **half their body fat** to stay warm and healthy.

## CITY SLICKERS VS. COUNTRY EXPLORERS

Raccoons that live in cities are like little geniuses compared to their country cousins. Scientists have

City life? Fine by me!

found that city raccoons are faster at solving puzzles, probably because they've had to figure out how to open garbage cans, sneak past fences, and outsmart curious humans. City raccoons also stay up later and sleep longer, adjusting their schedules to match the quietest times in the city. Meanwhile, raccoons in forests stick to their more traditional nighttime schedule.

## MEMORY MAPS: BUILT-IN GPS

Raccoons have incredible memories that help them navigate their world like little furry GPS systems. They create mental maps of their territory and can remember the exact locations of food, water, and cozy sleeping spots for **years.** They even remember which trees have the best hiding places and which neighborhood dogs are friendly—*or not-so-friendly*! With a memory like that, raccoons never forget where to find their next snack.

## SECRET MOM-AND-BABY CODE

Mother raccoons have their own unique way of communicating with their babies—as if they have a secret language only they can understand! They use different sounds to call their kits, and each baby raccoon can recognize its mom's unique voice. Even in a big group of raccoons, a kit can tell exactly which sound belongs to its mom. It's like having a one-of-a-kind ringtone that only you can hear!

These fantastic facts show how clever, tough, and adaptable raccoons really are. And guess what? Scientists are still discovering new things about these incredible animals every day. So the next time you spot a raccoon sneaking through the trees or exploring a backyard, remember—you're looking at one of nature's most brilliant little adventurers!

We're always up for an adventure!

# CONGRATULATIONS!
## YOU'RE NOW A RACCOON EXPERT!

Wow! What an adventure we've had exploring the world of raccoons! From their clever hands to their problem-solving brains, you've discovered why these masked bandits are some of the most fascinating animals in nature.

You now know that raccoons are more than just sneaky nighttime visitors—they're smart, adaptable survivors who can make a home just about anywhere. With their super-sensitive hands, fantastic memories, and curious minds, they've learned how to thrive in both wild forests and busy cities. Whether climbing trees, fishing in streams, or solving puzzles to open lids and locks, raccoons are true experts at exploring their world.

Now that you're a certified raccoon expert, you can also help others understand these clever creatures! Remember, even though raccoons might sometimes cause a little bit of trouble in our neighborhoods,

they're still wild animals and deserve our respect and kindness. Watching them from a safe distance is the best way to enjoy their curious antics while keeping both them and us safe.

Thank you for joining us on this exciting journey into the world of raccoons. Now go out and share your raccoon wisdom with the world—you never know when someone might need a raccoon expert like you!

# IT'S TIME TO PAWS
## AND APPRECIATE RACOONS!

# THANK YOU!

Thank you for reading this book and for allowing us to share our love for raccoons with you!

If you've enjoyed this book, please let us know by leaving a rating and a brief review wherever you made your purchase! This helps us spread the word to other readers!

Thank you for your time, and have an awesome day!

For more information, please visit:
**www.animalreads.com**

© Copyright 2025—All rights reserved Admore Publishing

ISBN: 978-3-96772-191-1

ISBN: 978-3-96772-192-8

ISBN: 978-3-96772-193-5

Animal Reads at www.animalreads.com

The content contained within this book may not be reproduced, duplicated or transmitted without direct written permission from the author or the publisher.

Under no circumstances will any blame or legal responsibility be held against the publisher, or author, for any damages, reparation, or monetary loss due to the information contained within this book. Either directly or indirectly.

Published by Admore Publishing: Gotenstraße, Berlin, Germany

www.admorepublishing.com

www.ingramcontent.com/pod-product-compliance
Lightning Source LLC
LaVergne TN
LVHW021340080526
838202LV00004B/250